THE GREAT
YELLOWSTONE
GRAND TETON
GLACIER
ACTIVITY BOOK

rising moon

The Great Yellowstone, Grand Teton, Glacier Activity Book
© 2004 by Rising Moon
Illustrations © 2004 by:
David Brooks: 3, 11, 17, 21, 28-29, 30, 35, 40, 42, 46, 49
Mike Gordon: 5, 6, 8, 18, 32, 34, 38, 46
Peter Grosshauser: 10, 15, 16, 19, 23, 26, 40, 41, 42, 43
Larry Jones: cover, 4, 12, 13, 20
Joe Marciniak: 8, 22, 27, 37, 39, 44-45
Bill Perry: 47
Chris Sabatino: 4, 14, 24, 33

www.northlandbooks.com

Composed in the United States of America
Printed in China

Edited by Theresa Howell
Designed by Katie Jennings
Production supervised by Donna Boyd

Huizhou,Guangdong,PRC,China
Date of Production: May/03/2011
Cohort: Batch 1

FIRST IMPRESSION 2004
ISBN 13: 978-0-87358-860-7
ISBN 10: 0-87358-860-6

POSTCARD MATCH UP

Some of the postcards these travelers sent back home to friends got mixed up in the mail. See if you can straighten things out by drawing a line from the picture on the front of the postcard to the matching note on the back.

Dear Carl,

We went swimming in Jackson Lake. The water was cold, but it was fun!

Susan

Dear Mary,

Did you know that a geyser is caused by boiling water exploding from the earth's surface. It's radical!

Monica

Dear Eric,

We spent the night at the Many Glacier Hotel. Wow!

Inna

3

ANIMAL SCRAMBLE

These animals are all mixed up. Unscramble the names of the animals below.
Have you seen any of these animals on your trip?

1. seomo _____

2. lke _____

3. tommar _____

4. sonib _____

5. legae _____

6. xynl _____

7. zzlygir earb _____

8. pinkhucm _____

Did you know that a moose can weigh over one thousand (1000) pounds?

MOOSE · LYNX · ELK · BISON · EAGLE
GRIZZLY BEAR · CHIPMUNK · MARMOT

4

I'M GOING TO A NATIONAL PARK AND I'M GOING TO PACK....

This is a two-part activity. First things first—you're going to a national park and you need to pack. The tricky part is that there's just enough room in the car for you to take one thing for every letter of the alphabet. Take a good hard look at the picture below and mark each item on this page by what letter it starts with.

Next, turn the page and write your list from memory.

DON'T TURN BACK!

I'M GOING TO A NATIONAL PARK AND I'M GOING TO PACK...

Can you remember all of the things you're bringing to the national parks?
Write a list of what you decided to pack from A to Z.

DON'T TURN BACK!

A _____
B _____
C _____
D _____
E _____
F _____
G _____
H _____
I _____
J _____
K _____
L _____
M _____
N _____
O _____
P _____
Q _____
R _____
S _____
T _____
U _____
V _____
W _____
X _____
Y _____
Z _____

CAR TRIP TIP

While you're riding in the car you can play this game with your family and friends. Start off with something that begins with the letter **A**. For example, you might say, *"I'm going to the national parks and I'm going to bring an armadillo."* The next person repeats what you said but adds something that starts with the letter **B**. Continue on until you've gone through the whole alphabet. Now that's a good memory!

I SPY A RAINBOW

GREEN   RED   PINK
TURQUOISE   ORANGE   BLACK
BROWN   BLUE   WHITE   PURPLE
YELLOW

Glacier, Grand Teton, and Yellowstone National Parks are colorful places. See how many things you can find for each of these colors just by looking out your window. Write a list below.

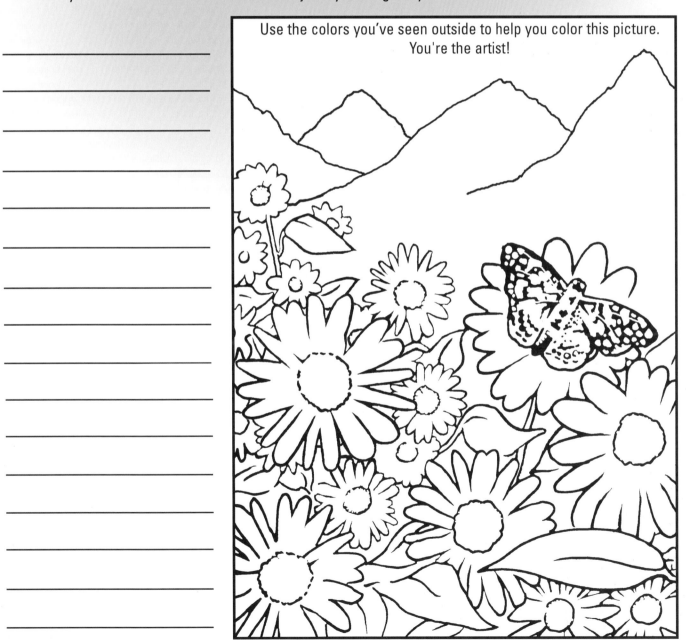

Use the colors you've seen outside to help you color this picture.
You're the artist!

_____
_____
_____
_____
_____
_____
_____
_____
_____
_____
_____
_____
_____
_____
_____

MYSTERY MEADOW

Can you find the butterfly, bumblebee, mushroom, rabbit, paintbrush, bird, sun, picnic basket, and snake hidden in or around the meadow at Grand Teton National Park?

IT'S A BIG ONE!

What did this lucky angler pull out of the water? Connect the dots to find out.

NATIONAL PARK PICTURE PUZZLE

Use the pictures below to name some of the amazing plants, animals, and features you might see in Yellowstone, Grand Teton, and Glacier National Parks.

1.  + = _____ _____

2. + 2000 LBS. (ton) + + = _____ _____

3. K + + O + = _____

4. + = _____

5. + = _____

6. + N + = _____ _____

7. B + + = _____

8. + = _____ _____

GLACIER WORD FIND

Find the words on the side of this red van in the word find puzzle.

```
S W I F T C U R R E N T L A K E S A M H B
H E C F C G S H F R J C H Y Q W T G O E L
I E S B T R D F G V H D J X K L M X U A O
D P N P B E A R H A T M O U N T A I N V G
D I M V Q W S X G Y R Z B C P D R W T E A
E N R B D R G F J Q W K J N L T Y M S N N
N G R I N N E L L G L A C I E R L P I S P
L W L N B P D F Q H X Y R K S L A Z Y P A
A A P P E K U N N Y F A L L S N K V E E S
K L Z M V T W V H J X S Y T M B E P H A S
E L A K E M C D O N A L D L Z Y C K N K Z
```

HIDDEN LAKE · SWIFTCURRENT LAKE · WEEPING WALL
LAKE MCDONALD · APPEKUNNY FALLS · LOGAN PASS
ST. MARY LAKE · MOUNT SIYEH · GRINNELL GLACIER
BEARHAT MOUNTAIN · HEAVENS PEAK

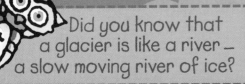

Did you know that a glacier is like a river — a slow moving river of ice?

BEAR TROUBLE

Don't feed the bears in the national park!
Can you make it all the way back to your tent
without disturbing a single bear?

12

COWBOY CODE BREAKER

Use the key to discover a cowboy's #1 rule.

A B C D F G H I J K L M

N O P Q R S T U V W Y

,

!

Number the scenes below to show what happened first, second, and so on during the mountain goats' train trip to Glacier National Park.

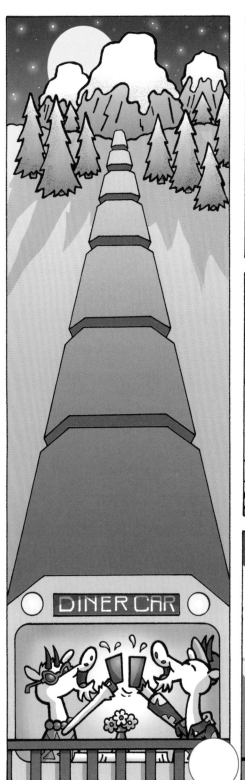

MY NATIONAL PARK VACATION

You and a travel buddy can create your own version of your national park vacation.
① Don't let your buddy see this page and don't read the story out loud—yet.
② Ask him or her for words to fill in the blanks of the story. Use the words below the blanks as a guide.
③ When you've finished, read the story out loud and find out just how crazy your vacation could actually be.

This summer _____ and I went to _____. As soon
           (person's name)   *(a national park)*

as we got there I realized that I forgot to pack my _____.
                                                        (a thing)

I brought my_____ by accident. It didn't really matter though
            (a thing)

because we spent _____ weeks _____ and _____.
                      (number)   *(–ing word)*   *(–ing word)*

One day we saw a_____ from the car window. We started
                (an animal)

_____. On our trip we ate _____ almost every day for
  (–ing word)   *(a food)*

lunch. It was _____. I'm going to remember this
              (describing word)

vacation forever! I took lots and lots of _____ and bought
                                              (things)

a souvenir_____ .
          (a thing)

GRAND TETON WORD FIND

Find these places hidden in Jackson Lake.

THOR PEAK
ELK ISLAND
MOUNT MORAN
LAKE SOLITUDE
TABLE MOUNTAIN
CASCADE CANYON
RENDEZVOUS MOUNTAIN

JENNY LAKE
SNAKE RIVER
JACKSON RIVER
CATHEDRAL GROUP
GROS VENTRE RIVER
AVALANCHE CANYON

```
B F S E G T C J V C H W G D H X C
R M O U N T M O R A N L B N J M V
E Q V M J D T X S T R S Q Y B H P
N W C N E X L Y K H M Z A G T C Z
D P M D N Z A J B E K R A L J A B
E T C R N F K F L D L G V F C S H
Z M S L Y V E W N R M X A K J C Y
V D F G L H S P V A Q B L Z K A R
O R S M A D O F J L K Q A R J D Z
U F P N K R L K L G T Y N Q A E V
S N A K E R I V E R K W C D C C E
M X P C Q C T B H O G P H Y K A T
O N N D M D U P N U L M E L S N V
U Z B C C S D F J P F R C X O Y S
N T H O R P E A K W G W A D N O B
T A B L E M O U N T A I N H R N W
A Q Z N T H C S H V X J Y K I M F
I P P J B U G J V G T Q O W V X L
N B Z R Q E L K I S L A N D E G Y
G R O S V E N T R E R I V E R K F
```

DOUBLE TAKE!

Look carefully. There are ten differences between these two pictures of a family at the Old Faithful Geyser. Can you spot them? Circle the differences in the bottom picture.

CURIOS

Help these kids pick out a few souvenirs to bring back home. They have exactly 105 tickets to spend in the curios shop. They can't spend a ticket more or a ticket less. Add it up—what goodies can they buy?

PARK STORE

ANIMALS
30
tickets

SHIRTS
45
tickets

POSTCARDS
5
tickets

HATS
75
tickets

YELLOWSTONE

ACTIVITY BOOK

BOOKS
25 tickets

DON'T FEED THE BEARS

DON'T FEED THE BEARS!

SHERIFF BADGE
35
tickets

SNOW GLOBES
50
tickets

SCRATCH PAD

POSTCARD EXPRESS

Draw a picture of your favorite thing you've seen on your trip. On the opposite side of the postcard, write a friend all about it.

★ NATURAL WONDERS ★

Each of these natural wonders will fit into one spot and one spot only in this puzzle.
See if you can place each of these WONDERful features where it belongs.

WATERFALL   MOUNTAIN
FUMAROLE   GEYSER
GLACIER   HOT SPRINGS
RIVER   CANYON
LAKE   MUD POT
PAINT POT

NATURALWONDERS

Did you know that fumaroles are vents in the earth's surface where steam and gasses shoot out?

LEAVE NO TRACE

This is an important rule to remember when you're out on the trail. Use the symbols below to get the message.

A	B	C	D	E	F	G	H	I	J	K	L	M	N

O	P	Q	R	S	T	U	V	W	X	Y	Z

TAKE ONLY

PICTURES.

LEAVE ONLY

FOOTPRINTS.

OVERBOARD

See if you can find the sunglasses, cooler, soda can, sandal, swim trunks, hot dog, guitar, frying pan, tent, fishing pole, sun hat, suntan lotion, and flashlight in this picture of folks having fun on a Grand Teton scenic rafting trip. Remember to be more careful than these guys, and don't drop anything in the river!

CRAZY CAMP

Number the scenes below to show what happened first, second, and so on during this family's camping trip to the park.

BALDY

The turkey was almost chosen as the national bird of the United States of America.
Connect the dots to find out which bird was actually chosen.

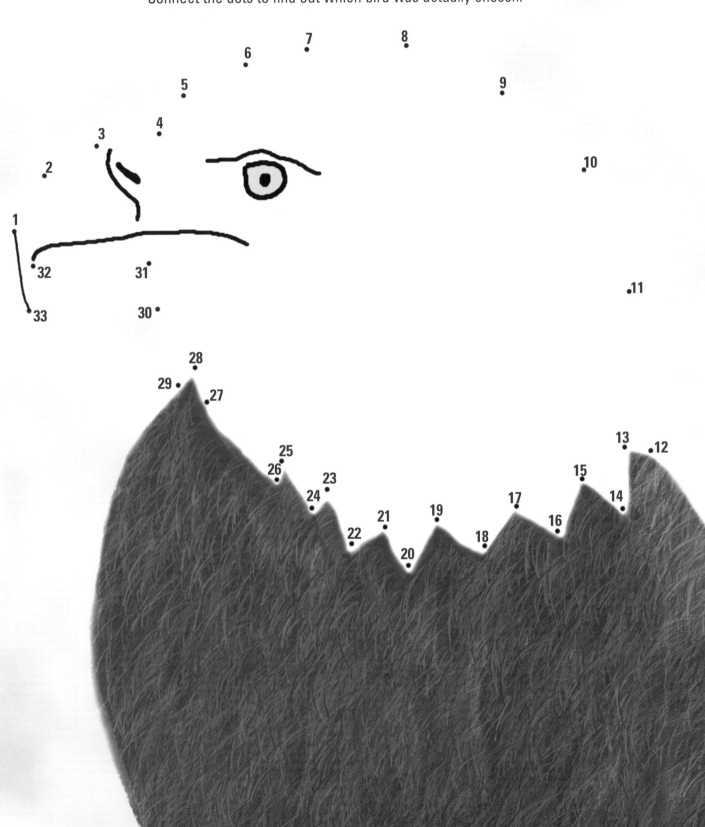

ANIMAL TRACKS MAZE

These animals left their tracks behind.
Match the bison, the coyote, the elk, and the bear with the correct set of tracks.

YELLOWSTONE WORD FIND

Find these places hidden in the puzzle in Lower Falls.

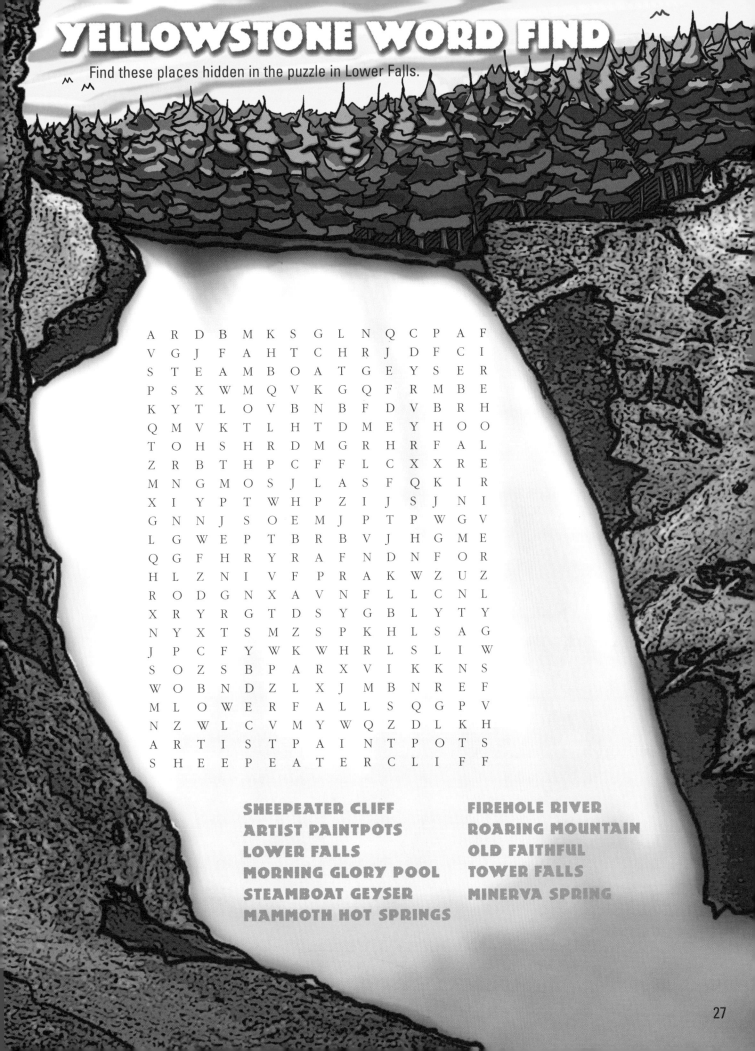

```
A R D B M K S G L N Q C P A F
V G J F A H T C H R J D F C I
S T E A M B O A T G E Y S E R
P S X W M Q V K G Q F R M B E
K Y T L O V B N B F D V B R H
Q M V K T L H T D M E Y H O O
T O H S H R D M G R H R F A L
Z R B T H P C F F L C X X R E
M N G M O S J L A S F Q K I R
X I Y P T W H P Z I J S J N I
G N N J S O E M J P T P W G V
L G W E P T B R B V J H G M E
Q G F H R Y R A F N D N F O R
H L Z N I V F P R A K W Z U Z
R O D G N X A V N F L L C N L
X R Y R G T D S Y G B L Y T Y
N Y X T S M Z S P K H L S A G
J P C F Y W K W H R L L S L I W
S O Z S B P A R X V I K K N S
W O B N D Z L X J M B N R E F
M L O W E R F A L L S Q G P V
N Z W L C V M Y W Q Z D L K H
A R T I S T P A I N T P O T S
S H E E P E A T E R C L I F F
```

SHEEPEATER CLIFF　　　**FIREHOLE RIVER**
ARTIST PAINTPOTS　　　**ROARING MOUNTAIN**
LOWER FALLS　　　　　　**OLD FAITHFUL**
MORNING GLORY POOL　　**TOWER FALLS**
STEAMBOAT GEYSER　　　**MINERVA SPRING**
MAMMOTH HOT SPRINGS

TRAVEL BINGO

Bingo is the name of this game-o. On your road trip from park to park try this. Here's how it works. You and another player each pick a board. Look out your window and mark the picture on your board if you spot it outside. Some things can be found inside the park, some things outside. The first person to spot five things in a row—down, across, or diagonally—wins!

ROUND 'EM UP!

H O W D Y P A R T N E R

Help this cowboy round up these stragglin' words. Each word has one spot in the puzzle above. See if you can get them all in line.
HINT: The spaces between the words don't count.

Cattle drive
Stirrup
Campfire
Horseshoe
Brand
Bedroll
Lariat
Buckaroo
Chuck wagon
Guitar
Vaquero

Things I Saw

TRAVEL LOG

Use these notepads to record some of the high points
(or low points) on your national park vacation.

★ My Favorite Day

Things I Did

My Least Favorite Day

WHAT'S HIDDEN AT HIDDEN LAKE?

Can you spot the fish, ice axe, pinecone, fish hook, float tube, umbrella, camera, hiking boot, baby bear, and teepee hidden at Hidden Lake?

Circle 7 things that these careless park visitors are doing wrong.

PRETTY PARK PLANTS WORD FIND

Find the names of these plants, flowers, and trees
that help to make the parks beautiful.

```
B K Z F S E L K T H I S T L E M Y J
T C Y D H F N S W R V M F G X K P L
H R J K G L A G U R A N A I T N E G
L N A X D Q P I F Q R S H Q J R T L
O M S B V W P H R T Y W P S X L X A
D V R A B B H S C Y R D Y E D H F C
G B J L C I G V B J S G P A N K W I
E L V S M L T R N F R L Q N S M T E
P T V A D K V B F W P X I N L Z Y R
O Z J M H B Q E R C F D Y P U G M L
L S C R L G B G L U N N K Q P R L I
E H L O J Z K A M V S C P Z I E S L
P T F O P M V S W J Y H X B N D R Y
I E H T Z T H M B Y C X H J E K S C
N M O D N X W D G C O L U M B I N E
E T F W P A I N T B R U S H N C F I
B E A R G R A S S R B D I F G Z P B
K S N P J L Q C R F I R E W E E D Q
```

COLUMBINE

GLACIER LILY

LUPINE

PAINTBRUSH

FAIRYSLIPPER

ELK THISTLE

RABBIT BRUSH

BEARGRASS

BALSAM ROOT

LODGEPOLE PINE

FIREWEED

BEAR JAM

Number the scenes below to show what happened first, second, and so on when this family spots a bear on their trip to Yellowstone National Park.

BEARLY THERE

Who is climbing up this tree? Connect the dots to find out.

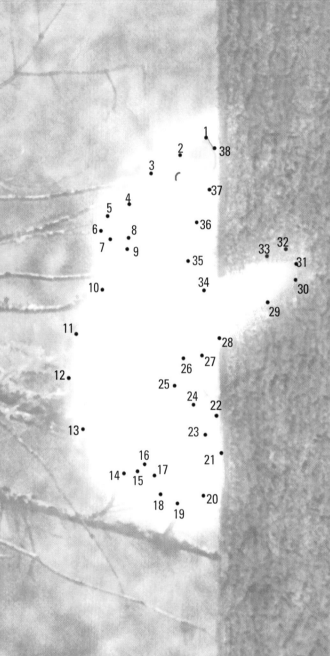

CRAZY CRITTERS

The jackelope is a mythical creature in the West. By all accounts he's a combination between a jackrabbit and an antelope—a funny-looking fellow. Who knows what else might be running around out there!

JACKRABBIT + ANTELOPE=
JACKELOPE

Can you think of names for these other imaginary animals?
Use the words below to create names for these funny-looking fellows.

BEAR · COYOTE · GOOSE · ANTELOPE · MOOSE · BUFFALO

_____   _____   _____

Now draw some of your own.
How about a foxupine (fox and porcupine) or a raccoonican (raccoon and pelican)?

SURVIVOR!

The national parks recommend bringing certain things when you spend time in the woods. This girl packed too much stuff for her camping trip. See if you can help her decide the 10 most important things to bring while spending time in the great outdoors.

MATCH IT

Match the color-coded places at the bottom of the page with the park it belongs in. Write the name of the place in the column with the same color. Yellowstone is yellow. Grand Teton is blue. Glacier is red.
Circle the places you have visited.

YELLOWSTONE

GRAND TETON

GLACIER

LAKE SOLITUDE   GOING TO THE SUN ROAD

LAKE MCDONALD   DRAGON'S MOUTH

JACKSON LAKE   MOUNT SIYEH   GROS VENTRE RIVER

LEWIS FALLS

ST. MARY LAKE   GRINNEL GLACIER   SNAKE RIVER   OLD FAITHFUL

MORNING GLORY POOL   MINERVA SPRING   THE GRAND TETON

A MAMMOTH OF A GOOD TIME

See if you can find the painter's palette, elephant, angel, wire spring, canary, sun, thermometer, table, and antler hidden in Mammoth Hot Springs at Yellowstone National Park.

PARK BABIES

There are special names for adult animals and their babies.
Draw lines from the name for the baby to the name for the mama or papa animal.

BEAR   KITTEN

MOUNTAIN LION   CUB

WOLF   TADPOLE

GOOSE   FAWN

BISON   CALF

DEER   EAGLET

EAGLE   PUP

SPOTTED FROG   GOSLING

HAPPY CAMPERS

```
E Q T D S A G B S M O R E S
T V C N S B X R F L O R M Q J L
W C A R W A D M V E T N K I C D
Y U A N H M C Z U A E X L G S A K B
S C B T F C K C L Z P F H M S M F L G
A T G E E B P L V Y I W K H Y P G J F
E F D C E B R A H M I N J E H N F P D L
H Y R X Q N G Q C X I W G N T O K I W K P Q
X G T L P J H I K I N G B O O T S R O D V C
M C M E N P D A W R S H P A R G D Z E T M Y V X
W S Z N F O F L A S H L I G H T O P R Z B Z Z J
B H W T N S N J T N V K O Q X B G M A T C H E S
```

Find the words below hidden in the tent.

WATER

FLASHLIGHT

S'MORES

SONGS

TENT

SLEEPING BAG

MATCHES

MAP

HIKING BOOTS

CANTEEN

BACKPACK

HOT DOG

CAMPFIRE

43

START

45

NATIONAL PARKS ARE FUN! CROSSWORD PUZZLE

DOWN

1. See how many _____ you can spot—bears, moose, bison.
2. Who's going to paddle when we go _____?
4. It's noon. We're hungry. Let's eat _____ at the lodge.
6. Pitch your tent and _____.
8. Giddy up! Spend the day _____-back riding.
9. In the winter you can go cross-country _____.

ACROSS

3. Do you think we can hike to the top of this _____?
5. Pull out your camera and take a _____.
7. Cast your line and go _____.
10. Put on your boots and take a _____.
11. Pedal faster! Let's go for a _____ ride.

FLUTTER BY

What did this butterfly stop to take a rest on?
Connect the dots to find out.

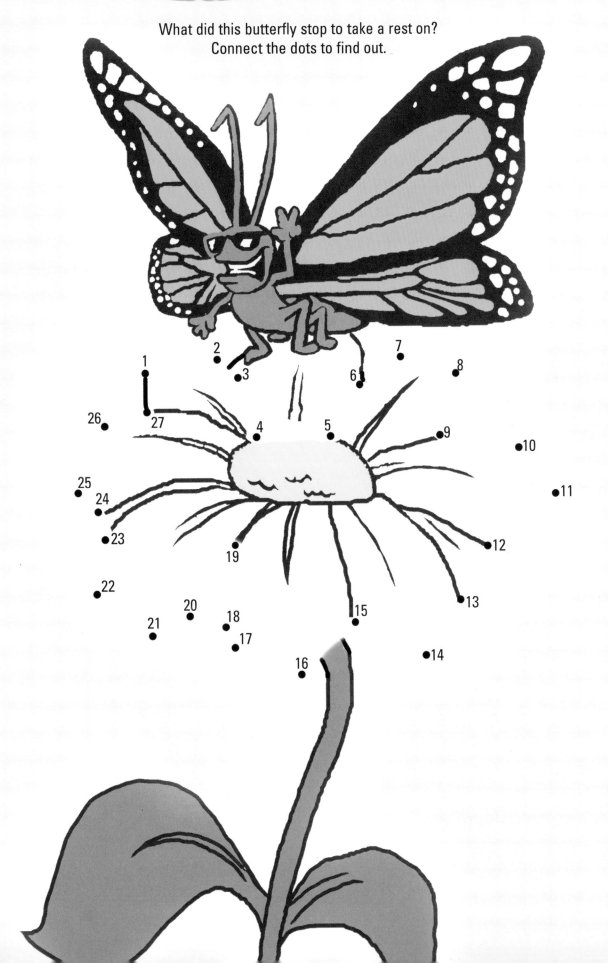

PARK FUN FACTS

See how much you learned about Glacier, Yellowstone, and Grand Teton National Parks.
Use the answers to the questions below to fill in the puzzle—all of the answers can be found in this book.
Feel free to go searching if you can't remember. At the end, you should be able to break the code.

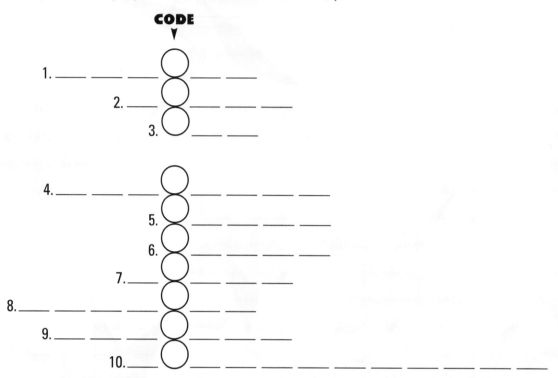

CODE

1. ___ ___ ___○___ ___
2. ___○___ ___ ___ ___
3. ___○___ ___

4. ___ ___ ___○___ ___ ___ ___ ___ ___
5. ___○___ ___ ___ ___
6. ___○___ ___ ___
7. ___○___ ___ ___ ___
8. ___ ___ ___ ___○___
9. ___ ___ ___ ___○___ ___ ___
10. ___○___ ___ ___ ___ ___ ___ ___ ___ ___

FUN FACTS

1. What is caused by boiling water exploding from the earth's surface? (page 3)

2. Whatever you do—don't feed the _____. (page 18)

3. Who do these prints belong to? (page 26)

4. What do you call a vent in the earth's surface that shoots out steam and gasses? (page 21)

5. This animal has big antlers and can weigh over 1000 pounds! (page 4)

6. This bird beat out the turkey as the national symbol of the United States. (page 25)

7. When hiking, always stay on the _____. (page 33)

8. What do you call a baby goose? (page 42)

9. What is like a slow moving river of ice? (page 11)

10. This flower is fit for a fairy. (page 34)

MY FAVORITE MEMORY

Draw your very own favorite memory of the national parks. It's like taking a picture.

SOLUTIONS

POSTCARD MATCH UP
(page 3)

ANIMAL SCRAMBLE
(page 4)

1. Moose
2. Elk
3. Marmot
4. Bison
5. Eagle
6. Lynx
7. Grizzly bear
8. Chipmunk

I'M GOING TO A NATIONAL PARK AND I'M GOING TO PACK...
(pages 5 and 6)

Apple	Jump rope	Sunglasses
Bowl	Knife	Toothbrush
Camera	Lantern	Umbrella
Dog	Map	Volleyball
Envelope	Net	Watch
Fishing Pole	Orange	Xylophone
Gloves	Pan	Yo-yo
Hat	Quilt	Zipper
Ice cream cone	Radio	

MYSTERY MEADOW
(page 8)

IT'S A BIG ONE!
(page 9)

A fish

NATIONAL PARK PICTURE PUZZLE
(page 10)

1. Hot spring
2. Cottonwood tree
3. Coyote
4. Waterfall
5. Cowboy
6. Pine tree
7. Bison
8. Mountain goat

SOLUTIONS

GLACIER WORD FIND
(page 11)

```
S W I F T C U R R E N T L A K E  S A M H B
H E C F C G S H F R J C H Y Q W  T G O E L
I E S B T R D F G V H D J X K L  M X U A O
D P N P B E A R H A T M O U N T  A I N V G
D I M V Q W S X G Y R Z B C P D  R W T E A
E N R B D R G F J Q W K J N L T  Y Y M S N
N G R I N N E L L G L A C I E R  L P I S P
L W L N B P D F Q H X Y R K S L  A Z Y P A
A A P P E K U N N Y F A L L S N  K V E E S
K L Z M V T W V H J X S Y T M B  E P H A S
E L A K E M C D O N A L D L Z Y  C K N K Z
```

OUT OF ORDER
(page 14)

BEAR TROUBLE
(page 12)

GRAND TETON WORD FIND
(page 16)

```
B F S E G T C J V C H W G D H X C
R Q V M J D T X S T R S Q N Y B M V
E W C N E X L Y K H M Z A G T C P Z
N P M D N Z A J B E K R G L F A C B
D T C R N F K F L D L G A F C S H Y
E M S L Y V K E W N M X V K Z C R Z
Z D F G L H S P V A Q B A L Z J A D V
V R S M A D O F J K K Q N R Q D E Z E
O F P N K L K L T Y A N C J C T V
S N A K E R I V E R K W H Q A K S B
M X P C Q C T B H O G P H Y L S N Y
O N N D M D P N U L M E L K O F
U Z B C C S D F J P F R X N V B
N T H O R P E A K W G W D H I W
T A B L E M O U N T A I N H K
A Q Z N T H C S H V X J Y N K M X
I P P J B U G J V G T Q O W L Y
N B Z R Q E L K I S L A N D G K F
G R O S V E N T R E R I V E R K F
```

COWBOY CODE BREAKER
(page 13)

Don't squat with your spurs on!

DOUBLE TAKE!
(page 17)

SOLUTIONS

CURIOS
(page 18)

With 105 tickets, the kids could buy:

a hat and a stuffed animal
    or
a hat, an activity book, and a postcard
    or
a tee-shirt, a sheriff's badge, and an activity book
    or
a snow globe, a stuffed animal, and an activity book

SOMETHING'S FISHY
(page 20)

NATURAL WONDERS
(page 21)

PAINTPOT
HOTSPRINGS
RIVER
MOUNTAIN
CANYON
GEYSER
LAKE
NATURALWONDERS
WATERFALL
FUMAROLE
GLACIER

LEAVE NO TRACE
(page 22)

Take only pictures. Leave only footprints.

OVERBOARD
(page 23)

CRAZY CAMP
(page 24)

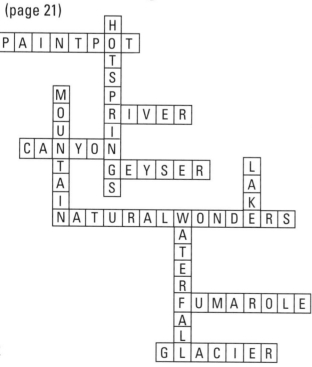

SOLUTIONS

BALDY
(page 25)

A bald eagle

ANIMAL TRACKS
(page 26)

YELLOWSTONE WORD FIND
(page 27)

ROUND 'EM UP!
(page 30)

SOLUTIONS

WHAT'S HIDDEN AT HIDDEN LAKE?
(page 32)

PRETTY PARK PLANTS WORD FIND
(page 34)

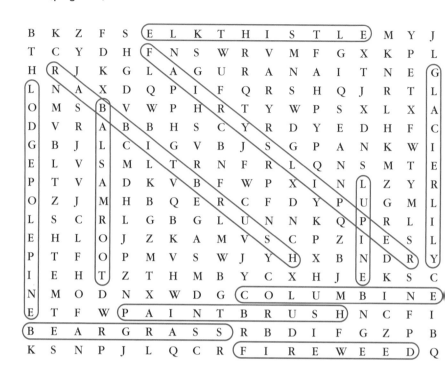

TROUBLESOME TRAILBLAZERS
(page 33)

BEAR JAM
(page 35)

BEARLY THERE
(page 36)

Black Bear

SOLUTIONS

CRAZY CRITTERS
(page 37)

[Possible solutions]

Bearyote • Goosalope • Moosalo

SURVIVOR!
(page 38)

Water
Compass
Raincoat
Knife
Extra shirt
Map

Flashlight
Matches
First Aid kit
Sunglasses

A FURRY FISH?
(page 39)

MATCH IT
(page 40)

Yellowstone- Morning Glory Pool, Minerva Springs, Lewis Falls, Dragon's Mouth, Old Faithful

Glacier- Lake McDonald, St. Mary Lake, Grinnel Glacier, Mount Siyeh, Going to the Sun Road

Grand Teton- Jackson Lake, Lake Solitude, Snake River, Gros Ventre River, the Grand Teton

A MAMMOTH OF A GOOD TIME
(page 41)

PARK BABIES
(page 42)

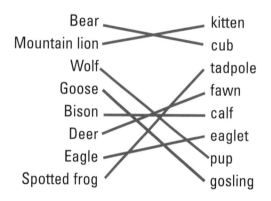

Bear — cub
Mountain lion — kitten
Wolf — pup
Goose — gosling
Bison — calf
Deer — fawn
Eagle — eaglet
Spotted frog — tadpole

HAPPY CAMPERS
(page 43)

SOLUTIONS

OLD FAITHFUL WON'T WAIT
(pages 44 and 45)

NATIONAL PARKS ARE FUN!
CROSSWORD PUZZLE
(page 46)

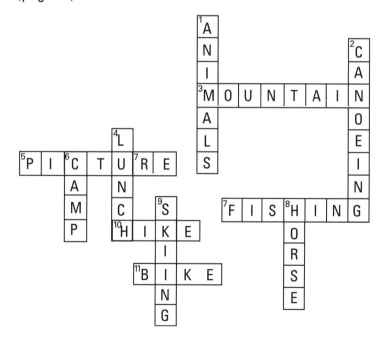

FLUTTER BY
(page 47)

A wildflower

PARK FUN FACTS
(page 48)

1. gey(S)er
2. b(e)ars
3. (e)lk
4. fum(a)role
5. (m)oose
6. (e)agle
7. t(r)ail
8. gosl(i)ng
9. gla(c)ier
10. f(a)iry slipper